Labyrinths and

Geoffrey Ashe

I shall show you the path which will take you home and I shall give wings to your mind that can carry you aloft . . .

BOETHIUS, Consolation of Philosophy, 524

Contents

WESSEX BOOKS

A Labyrinth or a Maze?

Labyrinths

Labyrinths and mazes are not the same. In practice, the terms are often used interchangeably, and it is hard to avoid an overlap. But their proper meanings contain a distinction that is rooted in history.

The word 'labyrinth' comes from Greek mythology. Strictly speaking, a labyrinth is *unicursal*. It is formed by a single path inside an enclosing boundary. Starting inwards from an entry point in the boundary, the path may twist and turn and double back, but it leads, normally, to a centre. Anyone who threads a human-sized labyrinth may have a long walk, but with perseverance the centre will be reached. A labyrinth, of course, can be reduced to a diagram with a plan of the same type, on which the single path can be traced visually.

This contemplative labyrinth in its woodland setting in Connecticut provides a peaceful place to remember the life of a much-loved son.

Mazes

Mazes are different. The word is related to 'amaze'. Chaucer, in his *Merchant's Tale* and elsewhere, speaks of people being 'mazed' or 'mazing', and this medieval usage suggests perplexity rather than surprise. A maze is *multicursal*. Like a labyrinth, it is enclosed by a boundary, and has a centre. But anyone trying to find the way to this confronts alternative paths from time to time, and must choose, because only one of them is right and the other leads to a dead end. A maze is a puzzle. A labyrinth is not.

There is a psychological difference. A maze-threader must concentrate on solving the puzzle. A labyrinth-threader has no such preoccupation, and the process of threading may be experienced as a meditation or ritual, or as symbolic of a long-drawn approach to some goal.

The Dragon Maze at Newquay Zoo, Cornwall, was designed by Randoll Coate and Adrian Fisher for children. The relatively low bushes of eleagnus allow children to see each other as they explore the passages which are in the shape of a dragon .

3

The classical story

The turf labyrinth at Saffron Walden is the largest ancient labyrinth in the British Isles. It measures about 120 feet (40 metres) across and the pathway is one mile long.

The word 'labyrinth' made its way into European languages from ancient Crete, where there was undoubtedly something called so, though it is not entirely clear what it was. The word may or may not be derived from *labrys*, meaning a kind of sacred axe, whatever the logic of the connection. According to legend, the Cretan king Minos had a wife named Pasiphaë. Thanks to some shady activities of the god Poseidon, she gave birth to the Minotaur, a semi-human creature with a bull's head. The master-craftsman Daedalus built a labyrinth — the original Labyrinth, prototype of all others — to hide the creature from the world. It was lodged at the centre, presumably with a chain or some other impediment to prevent it from wandering and getting out, and it devoured Athenian youths and maidens who were sent to Crete as an annual tribute. Instructed, however, by Ariadne, Minos's free-spirited daughter, the hero Theseus penetrated the Labyrinth and slew the Minotaur. Athens was freed from its obligation.

The minotaur in the labyrinth.

*Adrian Fisher designed
the Chinese Puzzle Maze
(opposite) on Blackpool
Pleasure Beach; two
bronze dragons spouting
jets of water guard the
hedge maze, whose goal
is a brightly painted
central tower.*

*St Mary Radcliffe Church,
Bristol has a roof boss in
the form of the medieval
Christian labyrinth, in
the north aisle.*

That is the classical story. But early clues indicate that the Labyrint
began, not as a building, but as the track followed in a ritual dance.
was a kind of spiral, but did not wind in towards the centre in simpl
lessening circles; it back tracked, running clockwise and counter
clockwise, inwards and outwards, in a devious approach. Dancers file
along the track, reached the centre at last, filed out again, and ende
by lining up outside.

Such a dance is known to have been performed, and not in Cret
alone. Theseus himself is said to have put in at the island of Delos o
his way home, and instituted the dance in honour of Apollo. Whateve
its true beginning, it was still being danced on Delos in historical time:
round Apollo's altar beside a lake. The Greek author Plutarch in th
first century AD describes it as 'an imitation of the circling passages i
the Labyrinth, consisting of certain rhythmic involutions and evolu
tions'. For some reason it was called the Crane Dance, but Plutarc
shows that its Cretan inspiration was recognised.

The Pattern

Dancing the labyrinth track

Dancers following the labyrinthine track would have been liable to get confused. So it would have been natural to mark out its pattern on the ground or a pavement. And that is the form which the Labyrinth seems to take, under Daedalus's hand, in the earliest literary reference to it. Homer is describing pictures worked by the god Hephaestus on a shield (Iliad XVIII.590 ff):

> The god depicted a dancing-floor like the one that Daedalus designed in the spacious town of Knossos for Ariadne of the lovely locks. Youths and marriageable maidens were dancing on it with their hands on one another's wrists. . . . Here they ran round, circling as smoothly on their accomplished feet as the wheel of a potter . . . and there they ran in lines to meet each other.

Veronica's Maze at Parham Park, West Sussex, is a path in grass maze with a one-way forwards rule. It was designed by Adrian Fisher for the late Veronica Tritton who used to play on this grass as a girl.

At some stage the pattern may have been given structural form in the royal palace, perhaps with elaborations to make it more impressive. The legend of Daedalus creating the Labyrinth as a building, to hide a monster, may then have grown around it. Glamis Castle in Scotland had a similar legend in modern times. But this is conjecture. Only the

original dance pattern is suggested by actual evidence. We can be fairly sure what it was, for two reasons.

In the first place, the course of the Labyrinth is depicted on Cretan coins. The path is a spiral, but a convoluted one. It starts inward from a gap in the perimeter. Instead of going to the centre directly, it makes a turn and goes nearly all the way round, then doubles back and goes round in the other direction, getting farther from the centre, not closer. After further alternations, still going in and out, it makes a final turn which at last brings it to the centre. In all, it makes seven circuits. Not complete ones, but an observer opposite the entrance would see a Labyrinth-threader pass seven times.

Knossos tablet.

The coins that show this design date only from the last three or four centuries BC. But an inscribed tablet from Knossos, fully a thousand years older, records an offering to a divine being called the Mistress of the Labyrinth. Ariadne may be a humanised form of her. Was her Labyrinth the same as the one on the coins?

Cretan, coincidental or sacred?

Septenary pattern

The second reason for accepting this septenary pattern is that we find it in other places, widely separated in space and time. There is a strong magic here. The pattern may be conveniently called 'Cretan', so long as the term is not taken to mean that other instances must all be derived from Crete. Its seven circuits are probably related to the ancient sacredness of that number, which is also widespread. The shape is sometimes round as on the coins, sometimes square. Its first circling may run clockwise or counter-clockwise, affecting the direction of the others accordingly. The pattern, however, is always basically the same. This backtracking path can be constructed geometrically if you know what you are trying to do, but the variations, the square versions, and the existence of crude and inaccurate early instances, make a neat geometrical origin seem questionable. There is no evidence that anybody in ancient times knew or used such a construction.

Bath Festival Maze, Beazer Gardens, Bath; 'The Maze' was chosen as the theme of the 1984 Bath International Music Festival, and this stone path-in-grass maze is that year's most enduring legacy in the landscape. It was designed by Adrian Fisher, and the central domed mosaic containing 92,000 pieces of Italian marble was created by Randoll Coate. The mosaic contains seven images relating to the city of Bath. One is the distinctive Minotaur mosaic (opposite) which provides the challenge to trace a labyrinthine mosaic path from one horn to the other — a veritable Gaze Maze.

The pattern appears in a square form on a tablet from Pylos in western Greece, dating from about 1200 BC. An even earlier tomb at Luzzanas in Sardinia has a rock carving of it. At Pompeii, on a crimson-painted pillar in a building called the House of Lucretius, the pattern is scratched – again in a square form – with the words LABYRINTHUS HIC HABITAT MINOTAURUS: 'the Labyrinth, here lives the Minotaur' – proof that this really was regarded as an image of the Minotaur's dwelling. The person who scratched it seemingly intended a gibe at the owner of the house.

The Minotaur

Pylos tablet.

From Ireland to India

The boulder in Hollywood, Co Wicklow.

Rocky Valley, Cornwall

Syria and the Caucasus Sri Lanka

Ireland supplies an instance from Hollywood, County Wicklow. In 1911, during the pursuit of a weasel, a granite boulder overturned, revealing a flat surface with the same labyrinth design carved on it, in circular form and about thirty inches across. According to Jeff Saward the design may be early Christian or as late as the fourteenth century. It is very difficult to date precisely. The boulder is now in Dublin's National Museum. In the Rocky Valley in Cornwall, which runs down to a bay near Tintagel, the round form of the pattern is carved twice on a vertical outcrop. These three examples are near early Christian sites, but not clearly associated with them. The Cornish carvings may be as early as 1000 BC, though this early dating has been challenged.

Eastward from Crete, examples occur in Syria and the Caucasus. Farther afield still, the pattern reappears in a manuscript illustration to the Indian epic *Ramayana*. It represents a fortress in Sri Lanka belonging to the demon Ravana, who abducts Sita, the wife of the hero Rama, and imprisons her in the fortress. Rama rescues her. The drawing is much later than the text, but the *Ramayana* says that when Rama and

One of the two seven-circuit classical labyrinths carved on a rockface in Rocky Valley, Tintagel, Cornwall. Each is 9 inches (23 cm) wide and can be seen at any time.

Michael Ayrton's Gravestone, Hadstock Churchyard, Essex; the image is that of the Arkville Maze which the English artist Michael Ayrton created in the Catskill Mountains, New York State.

ita were leaving Ravana's kingdom in his captured chariot, they ircled around the fortress seven times, a detail suggesting that it may lways have been imagined as septenary. The *Mahabharata*, the other reat Indian epic, introduces a similar labyrinth rather oddly as a attlefield formation designed to baffle an enemy army. A warrior who as learnt the secret penetrates it, but is lost and trapped. India has few on-literary examples, but there is one in the Ondavalli Temple in Andhra Pradesh.

Indian literary examples

A real Indian labyrinth

Tragliatella vase decoration

Hever Castle Hedge Maze, at Edenbridge in Kent, was planted in 1905 to recreate the Tudor setting where Henry VIII courted Anne Boleyn.

These instances are, so to speak, static. The mobility of the Cretan dance, however, was not confined to Crete. It appears in equestrian guise. An Etruscan vase found at Tragliatella in Italy, dating perhaps from the seventh century BC, has pictures on it that include two armed horsemen. Behind them is a diagram of the Cretan-type spiral. Inside its perimeter is the unexpected word TRUIA – Troy.

These vase images have to do with a ceremony portrayed in Virgil's Aeneid (V.545 – 603). The poet calls it the *Lusus Trojae* or Game of Troy, and describes an imagined performance by ancient Trojans, supposedly ancestors of the Romans. Three troops of mounted youths, each guided by a troop leader, go through a series of evolutions, combining and dividing. At a specified point Virgil speaks of them as 'riding right and left in intertwining circles', tracing the Cretan Labyrinth path. The name *Lusus Trojae*, and the whole passage, claim a Trojan origin for an actual Roman institution, familiar in the poet's own time. The complex ceremonial ride must have been difficult, but it was feasible with a large space, competent leaders, and probably markers on the ground.

Decorative brick paving in the form of four puzzle mazes designed by Adrian Fisher adorn the Abbotswood Shopping Centre, Yate, Gloucestershire.

Birth of *Lusus*

According to one theory, the *Lusus* had its birth in a ritual for the foundation of a city. The Romans performed it on other occasions than that, if perhaps with a persisting notion of magical protection. It is the intrusion of Troy that is mysterious. This cannot have been due solely to the Romans' ancestral legend, because the Etruscan vase is non-Roman and much earlier than Virgil. However, imperial Rome adopted the *Lusus* as a set-piece cavalry display. During the first century AD, Nero took part and later depicted it on a medal. It may have been performed at the dedication of Constantinople in 330, when the emperor Constantine re-founded the city as a new capital, and it seems to have survived into the reign of Justinian two centuries later.

Welsh shepherds and *Caerdroia*

Far from the imperial cities, the same septenary pattern was noticed by nineteenth-century folklorists in Wales, as a design that shepherds cut in turf, and boys challenged other boys to draw. While the dance motif had faded, the Trojan connection – however it had gotten attached – lingered on: the labyrinth was known as *Caerdroia*, and represented the Walls, or Citadel, of Troy. Britain, of course, had once been Roman territory. But even Scandinavia, beyond the imperial frontier, has labyrinths of small stones embedded in the ground, often on islands; and while the pattern varies, the local names for them include forms of 'Troy Town' such as *Trojeborg*. These northern labyrinths seem to express a notion of good luck. Fishermen used to arrange them temporarily for magical purposes, such as ensuring fair weather or a good catch. In Sweden they are said to have had protective functions, acting as charms against wolves, hostile gnomes, or insanity.

The symbolism of life

Do we find more sophisticated motives for setting up a Cretan-type labyrinth? It has been argued that it carried a symbolism of life, or death-and-rebirth. The journey inward to the centre was a closing-in; the return journey outward along the same path meant a new beginning, an advance into light and liberty. The early dance form of it may have been an initiatory ritual. Even the version in literary legend, with the centre occupied by the death-dealing Minotaur, might be construed in this way: Theseus goes in, slays the monster, and gives life to its prospective victims.

Another idea is that labyrinthine magic was associated with a goddess – the Mistress of the Labyrinth who is mentioned on the Cnossus tablet, with Ariadne as her human manifestation. Folk traditions in some countries install a figure at the labyrinth's centre who is not a male monster like the Minotaur, but a young woman who has to be reached or set free. In certain Scandinavian games a big labyrinth was marked out, a girl took her place at the centre, and a young man wishing to dance with her had to make his way through without stumbling or making a mistake. Two young men might run a race to the centre.

We confront these possibilities – or something like them – in an instance of the Cretan-type labyrinth which is alone in having a living myth still attached to it. The most sacred image of the Hopi in Arizona is the Mother Earth symbol. It occurs in two diagrammatic forms, one square and one round, and the round one is the Cretan-type labyrinth. Both stand for the womb of Mother Earth, the divine birth-giver, and in the round form the labyrinthine path represents the road prescribed for a human being on the way through life. To follow this is to attain spiritual rebirth through the eternal Mother.

The two diagrammatic forms of the sacred Hopi symbol.

This walk-through parting waterfall was designed by Adrian Fisher to guard the entrance to the Tudor Hedge Maze at Legoland, Windsor, Berkshire. Faint hearts may be discouraged; bold visitors walk straight up to the waterfall, which magically parts and allows them to enter without getting wet.

A Maze-like Labyrinth

Glastonbury Tor Maze

A reconstruction of the Glastonbury Tor Maze, showing how the Cretan pattern can be adapted to the contours of the hill. Practical evidence of the path's existence is the fact that it has been successfully followed by a very large number of maze-threaders, following instructions first published in 1979.

The Hopi instance is remarkable, not least because it occurs so far from the others, with no apparent linkage. Closer to home, and even more remarkable if the case for it is accepted, is the controversial 'Glastonbury Tor Maze'. Properly speaking this is another labyrinth, though its time-worn condition can make it puzzling (maze-like, in fact) for an unprepared visitor trying to trace the path.

The Tor is the highest of the hills around Glastonbury in Somerset. Its slopes are terraced in a formation that can be viewed as making the Cretan pattern in three dimensions, moulded to the shape of the hill. Despite erosion and destruction, the path can be traced through a to and-fro ascent going round the Tor. This theory is the only one of the various 'fringe' notions about Glastonbury that any archaeologists have been willing to take seriously. It is hard to believe that erosion, agricultural work, or any other cause of an accidental kind, could have created even the possibility of such a design; and critics of the theory have not produced another hill where the possibility exists. Philip Rahtz, the Tor's principal excavator, thought this labyrinth might be assigned to the era of great ritual works like Avebury.

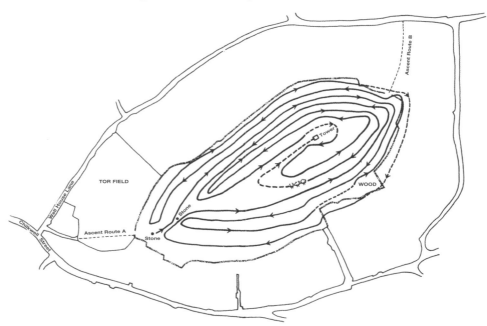

ongleat Hedge Maze, Longleat House, near Warminster, Wiltshire, was designed by Greg Bright in 1978.
This maze holds the world record for a permanent maze with the longest total path length.

Glastonbury has many religious associations, Christian and non-Christian, factual and legendary. Geoffrey Russell, who first suggested the Tor Maze, speculated that walking through it was a kind of pilgrimage to a ritual at the summit, and that this long, roundabout process was ancestral to the Quest of the Grail in Arthurian romance. Goddess-worship has also been proposed, and it could be significant that an early story about Queen Guinevere, which echoes pre-Christian myth, locates her at Glastonbury for a time. Rahtz's cautious but not unsympathetic conclusion was that 'if the maze theory were demonstrated to be true, it would clearly be of the greatest relevance to the origins of Glastonbury as a religious centre'.

Was Crete the starting point?

Did this recurrent motif spread through the world from a single country? The natural guess is that it did, and Crete itself was the starting-point. This, however, runs into difficulties with the Hopi, who are far away over the Pacific. Their mythology tells of past migrations, but not of ocean crossings. The Glastonbury Tor Maze, if that is real, raises another objection. Rahtz's dating would make it too early to be a product of Cretan influence.

Did the septenary labyrinth start in Asia?

An alternative view, far-fetched yet worth considering, is that the septenary labyrinth had its ancestry in north-central Asia – shamanic country. Religious and magical motifs did spread from there to other parts of the Old World, and if we look back to the time when Siberia and Alaska were joined, before 6000 BC, there could have been a similar spread with the wanderings of tribes that crossed the land bridge to people America. With the Cretan pattern, there may even be physical evidence for a Siberian ancestry. Objects retrieved from a cave-burial at Mal'ta, north-west of Irkutsk, include an oblong panel of mammoth ivory with lines of dots on it. These curl around forming simple designs. In a large design that completely dominates the rest, the line of dots goes spiralling into the centre of the panel, and it makes seven circuits. Here we have a septenary spiral much older than any other.

Admittedly this is a simple spiral, not a backtracking 'Cretan' one. If the Cretan type in its far-flung settings was the result of a simple one being diffused from a Siberian source, it would have had to grow more complex *en route*, in the hands of whatever shamans or priests made symbolic use of it. We might think that the end product would have been different in different places to which it spread. Actually this is not so. An American mathematician, Robert P. Thomas, has shown that there is only one symmetrical and elegant way to complicate a septenary spiral, and attempts to do so would quite likely have produced the Cretan pattern wherever they occured.

Mathematics gives a clue

In Europe, medieval authors describe labyrinths, with diagrams. These are still unicursal. Manuscripts relate them to real or legendary places. Jericho is sometimes portrayed on the Cretan plan, perhaps because of the Biblical story of Joshua's people marching round it seven times. However, medieval imagination opens a new chapter, breaking out from the septenary mould.

Jericho

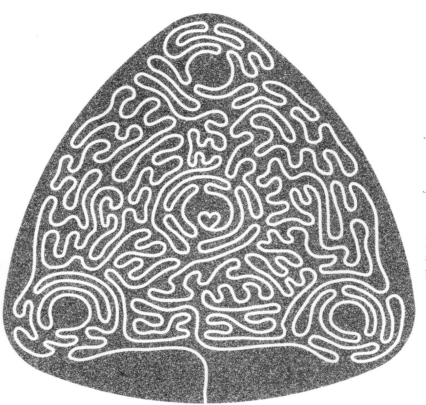

This is the plan of a labyrinth that was ploughed up at Pimperne, Dorset, in 1730. We have to thank the antiquarian John Aubrey for recording in 1686 that the path had been cut into the turf with one foot high ridges around it and that it was 'much used by the young people on Holydaies and by ye School-boies.'

The Medieval Labyrinth

Opposite page: *St Quentin Parish Church, northern France, 1495 AD. This distinctive octagonal stone pavement labyrinth measures 25 feet (8 metres) across and lies in the nave of the church. Its 11-ring design is one of the finest preserved examples of the ancient medieval Christian labyrinths.*

Hereford Cathedral's great Mappa Mundi or World Map belongs to the late thirteenth century. It represents Crete by a labyrinth design, as might be expected, but with eleven circuits, not seven. The pattern resembles one that was laid out on church pavements. Some of these labyrinths were demolished during the French Revolution, but some survived. Chartres Cathedral has a fine example dating from about 1260. It is formed by blue and white stones and is forty feet across. Its eleven-circuit path goes through bewildering convolutions.

Detail of Crete on the Mappa Mundi. Beside it is a copy of the whole of the Mappa Mundi, showing Crete less distinctly.

The purpose of threading

The Reims Cathedral plan.

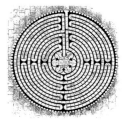

Chartres Cathedral plan.

Alkborough labyrinth (Julian's Bower). The earliest mention of this eleven-ring medieval Christian design is in the diary of Abraham de la Pryme 1671-1704 where it is 'nothing but (a) great labarinth'.

People presumably threaded these labyrinths, but no one knows why. According to one theory, the threading was penitential and may even have been performed on hands and knees. The journey inward symbolised involvement in earthly evil, the journey out symbolised recovery and redemption. That reading has some support from allegorical art portraying the world itself as labyrinthine. A complicated church labyrinth at St Omer, near Calais (see page 25), is supposed to have represented the road to Jerusalem. To make your way through it to the centre could have been a spiritual exercise in place of a real pilgrimage, though hardly equivalent.

Intriguingly, cathedrals at Sens and Auxerre staged 'Easter dances' in long-gone labyrinths resembling the one at Chartres. Another, in Reims Cathedral, was destroyed in 1779 by the order of a canon who disliked the noise made by children running round it during divine service. Whatever the original intention, it had become a place to play. And in fact, medieval Europe had non-religious labyrinths: pictures

how them in large gardens. Somewhat later, there are 'labyrinths of love' formed by hedges, perhaps with a maypole at the centre – a distant echo, if a coincidental one, of the Scandinavian dance custom. Perhaps a girl waited at the centre for a would-be lover; if not, how frustrating for him to get there and find only a maypole.

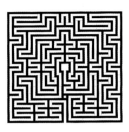

Less imposing, but still interesting, are labyrinths cut in turf in various parts of England. Many that existed once have been effaced by ploughing, or by plain neglect. But local care has preserved some survivors. These are apt to be close to churches. The local name may be 'the Maze' in some form, showing a blurring of distinctions.

St Omer labyrinth pattern, France, fourteenth century.

On a hillside at Alkborough in north Lincolnshire, near where the Ouse and Trent flow into the Humber, there is a round labyrinth known as Julian's Bower. In a shallow depression, it is about forty feet across, and partially – not completely – reproduces the Chartres pattern. Julian's Bower is thought to be medieval, and may have had some connection with a nearby monastery.

Mizmazes

Among trees on Breamore Down, north-west of Breamore House in Hampshire, is the 'Mizmaze'. This is similar to Julian's Bower, but bigger, being 87 feet (26.5 metres) across, with a large central area slightly higher than the surround. This too may have been associated with a monastery.

St Catherine's Hill near Winchester claims another 'Mizmaze', square in shape (see page 27).

A labyrinth at Comberton in Cambridgeshire was destroyed some 70 years ago. At Wing in Rutlandshire is an 'Old Maze' on the edge of the village green. Somerton in Oxfordshire, south of Banbury, has a big labyrinth called Troy-town. Its many convolutions have a total length

of 400 yards (365 metres). This one gives its name to the private property of which it is part, Troy Farm. It is not open to public gaze.

The labyrinth on St Catherine's Hill.

From Labyrinth to Maze

Saffron Walden in Essex has a labyrinth over a hundred feet (30 metres) across, with a pattern of its own (see page 5). Exceptional also is 'the Maze' at Hilton in Cambridgeshire. A little distance from the road, and slightly below ground level, it can be picked out as you approach by a square stone pillar at the centre with a globe on top. An inscription shows that it was made in 1660, perhaps as part of a celebration of the return of Charles II. In the 1920s the peculiarity of the Hilton design was that you could get from the entrance to the centre easily and quickly, but if you went on to explore further, you would run into complications. The Maze was tidied up in 1968 and now has one pathway again.

Turf Maze, Hilton Common, Cambridgeshire. The central stone pillar records that this turf maze was cut in 1660 by a certain William Sparrow, after the restoration of the monarchy.

Hardly any turf labyrinths reproduce the 'Cretan' pattern, even though it is simpler. However, there is one that does near Dalby in Yorkshire. About twenty feet (7 metres) across, it has been dubbed 'the Walls of Troy' or 'the City of Troy', like the comparable designs in Wales. As at Somerton, we are back with that unexplained Troy motif.

Is there an evolution?

Can we trace an evolution from unicursal labyrinths to multicursal mazes – that is, puzzles? Oddly, the notion of a puzzle is present by implication in the Cretan story itself, which has a strange ambiguity. If the Labyrinth was simply the backtracking spiral shown on coins and elsewhere, Theseus would have had a long walk to reach the Minotaur, but he would never have been in any doubt. We are told, nevertheless, that Ariadne had to explain the route, and that she gave him a thread to pay out behind him as he went, and follow as he retraced his steps. It is not clear why this aid was needed.

Was Daedalus original?

Some classical authors think Daedalus took a hint from an Egyptian temple-complex in Fayyum with many interconnecting chambers. This cannot be right, and it would explain nothing if it were. Yet the idea of difficulty persists when it is hard to see any reason for it. Two Roman poets who mention the Labyrinth confirm this ambiguity and seem not to realise what they are doing.

Ovid's view

Ovid compares its complexities to the windings of the River Meander (Menderes) in Asia Minor, a river from which the word 'meander' is derived. He describes the execution of Minos's edict that the Minotaur must be hidden:

> Daedalus, a man very famed for his skill in architecture, plans the work . . . and leads the eyes into mazy wanderings, by the intricacy of its various passages. . . . No otherwise than as the limpid Meander sports in the Phrygian fields, and flows backwards and forwards with its varying course . . . now pointing to its source, and now to the open sea: just so Daedalus fills innumerable paths with windings, and scarcely can he himself return to the entrance, so great are the intricacies of the place.

Ovid does not say that the 'innumerable paths' branched out from each other; he makes the winding river his simile. But mere 'windings' would not present a problem to Theseus or anyone else.

Virgil himself, in his narrative of the Game of Troy, also speaks of the Labyrinth as — in effect — a maze, even though the path followed by the riders is not a maze, as the Etruscan vase confirms. He says plainly that they go 'right and left in interwining circles', yet he says also:

> Once upon a time the Labyrinth in mountainous Crete contained a path, twining between walls which barred the view, with a treacherous uncertainty in its thousand ways, so that its baffling plan, which none might master and none retrace, would foil the trail of any guiding clues. By just such a course the sons of the Trojans knotted their paths.

This is peculiar, the more so as no riders, however skilful, could have imitated a sheer entanglement.

Tudor Rose Maze at Kentwell Hall, Long Melford, Suffolk, was created to celebrate the 500th accession of the Tudor dynasty, 1485–1985. The maze was designed by Adrian Fisher and the fifteen decorative diamonds were designed by Randoll Coate.

The symbolic hedge maze at Leeds Castle, near Maidstone, Kent, celebrates the three English Queens who lived at Leeds Castle. Its initial goal is a central stone tower. Beneath this tower, visitors experience a metamorphosis as they enter an underground grotto pictured on page 35.

An unwritten ambiguity

The ambiguity may be rooted in the first form of the Labyrinth, the dance. Performance in the open, without exact guidance, would have been tricky. The twistings in and out, back and forth, in the company of others, could easily have led to a mix-up. The Game of Troy on horseback would have had even more scope for error. Where the pattern was laid out on a marked track, or embodied in the plan of a building, the difficulty would have been removed. But a tradition of perplexity through mere convolution may have lingered, and an awareness that dancers or riders could take wrong turnings may have confused the Labyrinth's image and been compounded by later misunderstandings.

Mosaic labyrinthic patterns

Roman mosaic pavements, with labyrinthine patterns and pictures illustrating the Minotaur legend, have come to light in various places and some are so bewildering that they may show evolution in progress. But, for whatever reason, true multicursal mazes, with real wrong turnings built into them, take a long time to appear. They begin to do so at last during the fifteenth century and the beginnings of the European Renaissance.

A meditation tool

This development loses any symbolism of death-and-rebirth or new beginning. A labyrinth-threader, following a set path, can meditate on such themes. A maze-threader must concentrate on finding the way and this will be all the harder if the maze is a large one formed by walls or hedges that block vision, as in the well-known maze at Hampton Court.

The puzzle motif

A medieval legend, which was improved over the years, shows the puzzle motif taking shape in England. King Henry II (1133–1189) is said to have had a mistress, Rosamund Clifford, known as Fair Rosamund. To protect her from the jealous Queen Eleanor he installed her in a 'Bower' at Woodstock near Oxford. A central living-space was enclosed in an arrangement of hedges or walls. Some story-tellers describe it as a labyrinth with a single path, others as a true maze. The first notion came to be rejected, since the Queen would only have had to keep walking to reach the centre, and her rival would have had no escape route. A true maze would have been more effective, and that became the prevailing image. A ballad tells how Eleanor found the way nevertheless, and offered Rosamund a choice: she could die by a dagger or by poison. She chose poison. Slightly more credible is a version that has Rosamund concealed in a large, confusing house, like Elizabethan manors with their secret passages and priestholes. This too was improved upon; another ballad speaks absurdly of the Bower having 150 doors.

Rosamund is supposed, in reality, to have retired to a convent and died about 1176. Her legend became attached to a building near an old royal residence at Woodstock. This was still standing in the early eighteenth century, and could have been the large, confusing house of conjecture. Unfortunately it was pulled down during the construction of Blenheim Palace, and no description survives.

King David's Maize Maze, Elah Valley, Israel, for the 2001 season only. This Peace Maze drew 25,000 people in 8 weeks to the precise spot where David slew Goliath, alongside the brook from where David picked his 5 stones.

The Hedge Maze at Glendurgan House, near Falmouth, Cornwall, owned by the National Trust was originally planted in 1883. It has recently been restored and replanted.

Tennyson, in one of his little-known historical dramas (*Becket*), makes Fair Rosamund an important character. Here is Henry explaining the plan of the Bower:

> *See first, a circling wood,*
> *A hundred pathways running everyway,*
> *And then a brook, a bridge; and after that*
> *This labyrinthine brickwork maze in maze,*
> *And then another wood, and in the midst*
> *A garden and my Rosamund.*

In spite of all his efforts, Eleanor manages to get in.

Maze threaders at Leeds Castle follow a 30 metre (33 yards) underground tunnel in the grotto that provides a hidden quick exit out of the maze. Vernon Gibberd, Randoll Coate and Adrian Fisher designed the maze and grotto.

Rosamund's Bower, as a full-grown popular fiction, was inspired by large mazes that began to appear in the Renaissance, and enjoyed favour with the royalty and nobility of western Europe for several hundred years. Gardeners created dozens of them for employers who had the land and the money, though most were destroyed, sooner or later, to make way for alterations. High hedges or other arboreal barriers sometimes separated the paths, restricting visibility, so that guests who made their way in were suitably confused.

A French maze constructed in 1669 for the French King Louis XIV, in the grounds of the palace of Versailles, was not particularly complex, but the maze-threader was distracted by water jets and by statues illustrating Aesop's Fables, which had to be visited in the correct order. In Italy Pope Clement X, a contemporary, had an elaborate garden maze formed by tall box hedges. Best known of all is the hedge-maze at Hampton

Court Palace. This dates from 1690 when it was made for William III, who came from Holland where mazes were familiar, though it may have replaced an older one in the same area. It survived by becoming a public attraction. It has four sides, one of them 222 feet (67.5 metres) long. The total length of pathway is not actually great, but the complications are enough to get lost in. Benches at the centre provide a respite for the weary.

Labyrinths and mazes have their place in different schools of psychology. Jung noticed a tendency in his patients to dream about circling round a centre, which might or might not be reached, or to draw designs with a definite central point. He interpreted such imagery as symbolizing the psyche, with the centre representing what he called the Self, meaning its inmost nature – the true goal of the individual's quest in life, the key to vocation and psychological wholeness, to be identified through experience, reflection, perhaps analytic treatment. Jung drew a parallel with the mandalas or sacred designs of Buddhism, introduced by Kipling in his novel *Kim*. A labyrinth of the Cretan type or the Chartres type, where the circling process reaches the centre, can be a potent image of a process of self-discovery – an idea consistent with the 'rebirth' motif that appears, for instance, among the Hopi. Jean Houston, who conducted Mystery Schools in America, had the participants walk through a Cretan-type labyrinth as a meditative ritual. (I set up the first for her myself.)

The page opposite shows an example of eighteenth-century garden geometries.

Hampton Court Maze, Hampton Court Palace, Surrey was created in 1690 for William III.

Hampton Court Maze, Hampton Court Palace, Surrey, was created by command of King William III. It was designed and installed by George London and Henry Wise, 1690.

Psychologists of a more mundane kind have used mazes to make experiments in learning. If rats are put in a simple maze, which they must thread to get to food at the centre, they will start without a clue and wander at random. In successive tests they will eliminate the wrong turnings, find the shortest route, and stick to it thereafter. Some learn faster than others. That is probably due to nothing more mysterious than greater problem-solving skill. However, it has been alleged that the psychologist's attitude can affect performance. When a rat is mentally labelled 'good' it does better. Sceptics reluctant to admit

telepathy have argued that an experimenter with a favourite rat may make much of it and say, 'Who's a clever boy then?' or words to that effect – and the rat, encouraged, will outstrip its rivals. With or without the paranormal, rat behaviour in mazes is seemingly liable to confirm what physicists tell us in a different context: the experimenter is part of the experiment.

In a maze where the aim is to reach the centre, how can you find the way to it? Or to be precise, is there a systematic method of doing this, as distinct from wandering like an unpractised rat till you get lucky?

An eighteenth-century Chinese maze.

A famous fictional case of maze-solving, or rather non-solving, is in *Three Men in a Boat*, by Jerome K. Jerome. Its locale is the maze at Hampton Court, which in reality is neither very large nor exceptionally difficult, but, as the author knew, is capable of throwing visitors into total confusion. With good-natured exaggeration, he tells how Harris, one of the Three Men, approached it in a confident spirit to escort a visiting cousin. He had a method, and a map. *'It's absurd to call it a maze,' he said. 'You keep on taking the first turning to the right. We'll just walk round for ten minutes and then go and get some lunch.'*

Soon after they entered the maze, they met some people who had been there for three-quarters of an hour, and had had enough. Harris invited them to follow him. Presently he had a whole train of followers.

Harris kept on turning to the right, but it seemed a long way, and his cousin supposed it was a very big maze.

'Oh, one of the largest in Europe,' said Harris.

'Yes, it must be,' replied the cousin, 'because we've walked a good two miles already.'

Harris began to think it rather strange himself, but he held on until, at last, they passed the half of a penny bun on the ground that Harris's cousin swore he had noticed seven minutes ago . . .

He produced his map, and explained his theory.

'The map may be all right enough,' said one of the party, 'if you know whereabouts in it we are now.'

Harris didn't know, and suggested that the best thing to do would be to go back to the entrance, and begin again. For the beginning again part there was not much enthusiasm; but with regard to the advisability of going back to the entrance there was complete unanimity.

A few minutes later, however, they found themselves at the centre; and then they kept coming back to it.

Harris drew out his map again, after a while, but the sight of it only infuriated the mob, and they told him to go and curl his hair with it.

At last they shouted to attract the attention of the keeper, and he climbed a ladder outside and tried to direct them, but they only got muddled, and so did he. They were rescued finally by another keeper who knew the maze better.

The Old Palace, Hatfield House, Hatfield, Hertfordshire.

How to get through a maze

Actually, Harris was correct about turning to the right, and if he had stuck to that resolutely, he would have got through the maze. Maybe he would have done better without the map. The procedure can be made to work, though it calls for patience. In a maze like the one at Hampton Court, you can follow it, in effect, by keeping a hand continually on the hedge to your right. The left will work equally, but, whichever you choose, the vital thing is to go on as you started and never switch hedges. You may be led into blind alleys, but if you persist, never losing touch with your chosen hedge, you will be led out of the blind alleys and can proceed. You will gradually traverse the whole maze, reaching the centre and passing through it in the course of your tour, and going on after that till you emerge. You can do the same if the maze is a diagram on paper and you follow the equivalent of the hedge with a pencil.

The low box maze at the Old Palace, Hatfield House was designed by Lady Salisbury.

However, there is one condition. The tour will only be complete if all the hedges are connected with each other, and with the outside. If any portions of the maze are separate from the rest, you will miss

them, and if the centre itself is enclosed by an isolated hedge or group of hedges, making it an 'island', you will miss that. So, if you want to design a maze that can really puzzle, locate the centre in an 'island', or better still, an 'island' inside another one.

Fashions changed, and for many years mazes existed chiefly as minor amusements in pleasure-gardens, or as puzzles on paper in books and magazines. But the tradition of the large-scale hedge system was kept alive here and there: for instance, at Chevening House in Kent, the residence of the Earls of Stanhope; at Hatfield House in Hertfordshire, where a rectangular maze of yew hedges, 174 FEET BY 108 (53 metres by 33), was reputedly put together for a visit by Queen Victoria; and on several American sites, notably in 1935 at Williamsburg, Virginia, in the grounds of the colonial Governor's Palace. The Chevening maze was constructed between 1816 AND 1830 by an Earl with mathematical interests, and it may have been the first that used 'islands' to thwart the hand-on-hedge technique. The later Hatfield maze also has 'islands'.

How to set a maze-puzzle

ANCIENT TURF MAZES

1 Breamore 'Miz Maze', Hampshire
2 Winchester 'Miz Maze', Hampshire
3 Saffron Walden Turf Maze, Essex
4 Hilton Maze, Cambridgeshire
5 Wing Maze, Leicestershire
6 Julian's Bower, Alkborough, South Humberside
7 'City of Troy', Dalby, Yorkshire

ANCIENT ROMAN MOSAIC

8 Caerleon-on-Usk, Gwent

ANCIENT MAP

9 Mappa Mundi, Hereford Cathedral

BRICK MAZE

10 Temple Newsam Maze, Leeds

CONCRETE PATH MAZE

11 Irvine Beach Maze, Ayrshire

CONCRETE WALL MAZE

12 Mayflower Park Maze, Southampton, Hampshire

COLOUR MAZE

13 Flambards, The Park, Cornwall

FOOTPRINT MAZE

14 Bicton Park Maze, Devon

GILDED MAZE

15 Watts Memorial Chapel, Compton, Surrey

GRAVESTONE CARVING

16 Hadstock Churchyard, Essex

HEDGE MAZES

17 Glendurgan Maze, Falmouth, Cornwall
18 Newquay Zoo 'Dragon Maze', Newquay, Cornwall
19 Dart Valley Railway Maze, Buckfastleigh, Devon
20 Longleat Maze, Warminster, Wiltshire
21 Manningford Maze, Wiltshire
22 Alice in Wonderland Maze, Hurn, Dorset
23 Rhinefield Maze, Hampshire
24 Blackgang Chine Maze, Isle of Wight
25 Hampton Court Palace, Surrey
26 Hever Castle, Edenbridge, Kent
27 Leeds Castle, Maidstone, Kent

28 Crystal Palace Maze, South London
29 Capel Manor Maze, Enfield, Middlesex
30 Mistley Place Maze, Manningtree, Essex
31 Hatfield House Box Maze, Hatfield, Hertfordshire
32 Springfield Maze, Spalding, Lincolnshire
33 Somerleyton Maze, Lowestoft, Suffolk
34 Chatsworth Maze, Derbyshire
35 Tatton Turf Maze, Knutsford, Cheshire
36 Wonderland Maze, Telford, Shropshire
37 Castle Bromwich Gardens Maze, West Midlands
38 Marlborough Maze, Blenheim Palace, Oxfordshire
39 Saxon Maze, Sonning Common, Berkshire
40 Jubilee Maze, Symonds Yat, Hereford & Worcester
41 Llangoed Maze, Hereford and Worcester
42 Burford House Maze, Tenbury Wells, Hereford and Worcester
43 Environmental Maze, Machynlleth, Powys
44 Worden Park Maze, Lancashire
45 Pleasure Beach Maze, Blackpool, Lancashire
46 Burton Agnes Hall Maze, Driffield, Lancashire
47 Victoria Park Maze, Scarborough, Yorkshire
48 Esplanade Maze, Scarborough, Yorkshire
49 Saltwell Park Maze, Tyne and Wear
50 Traquair Maze, Peebleshire

MODERN TURF MAZES

51 Lappa Maze, St Newlyn East, Cornwall
52 Parham Park, West Sussex
53 Chenies Manor Maze, Chenies, Berkshire
54 Milton Keynes Maze, Willens Lake, Berkshire
55 Doddington Maze, Lincolnshire
56 Warrington Turf Maze, Parkfield, Cheshire
57 Archbishops Maze, Greys Court, Oxfordshire
58 Bath Festival Maze, Bath, Somerset
59 Rosehill Quarry Labyrinth, Swansea, West Glamorgan

60 The Caterpillar Maze, Leighton Hall, Lancashire
61 Rocket Maze, Whitley Bay, Tyne and Wear
62 Finlaystone Maze, Langbank, Inverclyde

MOSAIC MAZE

63 Gospel Maze, Wyck Rissington, Gloucestershire

PAVEMENT MAZES

64 Itchen Stoke Maze, Hampshire
65 Bourne Church, Cambridgeshire
66 Ely Cathedral Maze, Cambridgeshire
67 Unicorn Rampant Maze, Worksop
68 'Mathematica', Leicester University
69 Batheaston Church, Somerset
70 Hull Pavement Maze, North Humberside
71 Kentwell Hall 'Tudor Rose Maze', Suffolk

ROCK CARVINGS

72 Rocky Valley, Tintagel, Cornwall

ROOF BOSS MAZE

73 Bristol Roof Boss Maze, Redcliffe Church, Somerset

STAINED GLASS WINDOW

74 Irvine Town Centre, Ayrshire

STAINED GLASS WINDOW AND GRAVESTONE

75 Alkborough Church, South Humberside

STONE LABYRINTHS ANCIENT

76 St Agnes, Scilly Isles

STONE LABYRINTHS POST WORLD WAR II

77 St Martins, Scilly Isles

TILE MAZE

78 Warren Street Underground Station, London

WALL OF MIRRORS

79 Mirror Maze, Wookey Hole Caves, Somerset

WALL MAZE

80 Snakes and Ladders Maze, Ragley Hall, Warwickshire

WATER MAZE IN BRICK CHANNEL

81 Bristol Water Maze, Bristol, Somerset

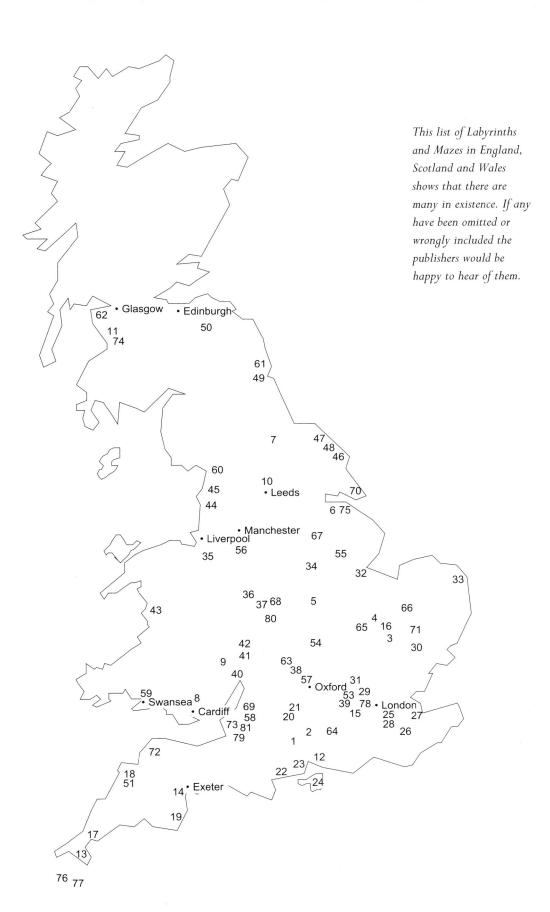

This list of Labyrinths and Mazes in England, Scotland and Wales shows that there are many in existence. If any have been omitted or wrongly included the publishers would be happy to hear of them.

• Glasgow   • Edinburgh
62   50

11
74

61
49

7   47
         48
          46

60
45   10   70
44   • Leeds
                        6 75

     • Manchester   67
• Liverpool
35   56   55
                34
                    32   33

36
37 68   5   66
80
                     4   71
43   65 16
                        3
                            30
42   54
41
9   63
40   38
        57 • Oxford 31
59   53 29
• Swansea 8   39 78 • London
• Cardiff 69   21   15 25   27
           58   20   28   26
        73 81   2   64
        79   1
72

18
51   23 12
        22   24
    14 • Exeter

        19

17

13

76 77

A Maze Revival

The Sun Maze and Lunar Labyrinth, designed by Randoll Coate for the Marquess of Bath at Longleat. The House is the best example of Elizabethan architecture in Britain and the grounds have several mazes and labyrinths. The Love Maze designed by Graham Burgess can be seen behind the House.

The last decades of the twentieth century witnessed a powerful revival mainly in England, the United States and Japan. In the 1970s at Longleat, the renowned 'stately home' with grounds open to the public, the Marquess of Bath commissioned an enormous hedge maze, planted by Greg Bright (see page 19). In 1991 Randoll Coate designed the huge Sun Maze and Lunar Labyrinth. His mosaic maze of original design was a lasting memento of the Bath Festival of 1984 (see pages 10, 11), in the gardens below Pulteney Bridge.

A few years later Dr Lauren Artress, a canon of Grace Cathedral in San Francisco, had a copy of the Chartres labyrinth painted on canvas and exhibited in the cathedral. This was presently replaced by a tapestry and a pavement labyrinth outside. Meanwhile dozens of mazes attested the popular interest, and by the turn of the twenty-first century there were more than sixty in England.

Lauren Artress was one of many who were looking at labyrinths from a psychological or spiritual point of view. One impulse came from fresh study of Glastonbury Tor, where the theory of a Cretan-type pattern appealed to increasing numbers. The Tor was given interpretations in terms of myth and ritual, which inspired meditative ascents by individual seekers and groups. Interest in the Tor helped to arouse interest in the septenary labyrinth generally: it was set up and walked through, even danced through, on American campuses, and proposed as a clue to neglected aspects of prehistoric culture.

Meanwhile maze-designing and maze-building became a recognised profession, with Adrian Fisher in Blandford Forum, England, as a leading exponent. Conferences attracted international audiences, and an English magazine, *Caerdroia*, flourishes as a clearing-house of information. Whatever it was that began so long ago, it could still weave an extraordinary spell.

WESSEX BOOKS

Some other Wessex Books include:

MERLIN Geoffrey Ashe

ARTHUR • LAND & LEGEND Kent Goodman

LEGENDS, MYTHS AND MAGIC Roger Crisp

CHALK FIGURES OF WESSEX Kent Goodman

PREHISTORIC SACRED SITES OF WESSEX Wingfield & Krönig

THOMAS HARDY Jane Drake

LEY LINES OF WESSEX Roger Crisp

PREHISTORIC SACRED SITES OF CORNWALL John Michell

BOSCASTLE Sheila Bird TINTAGEL Sheila Bird ST IVES Sheila Bird

ALFRED THE GREAT Douglas Stuckey

SIR CHRISTOPHER WREN Michael St John Parker

STONEHENGE, EARTH AND SKY Gerald Hawkins

CROP CIRCLES • AN INTRODUCTION Andy Thomas

IRON AGE CELTS in WESSEX David Allen

ROMANS in WESSEX Michael St John Parker

CROP CIRCLES • THE HIDDEN FORM Nick Kollerstrom

FURTHER READING

Ashe, Geoffrey, *Avalonian Quest*. Fontana, 1984.
———— *The Glastonbury Tor Maze,* Gothic Image Publications (Glastonbury), 1979; revised edition, 2001.
Dudeney, Henry Ernest, *Amusements in Mathematics*, Thomas Nelson, 1917.
Fisher, Adrian, and Georg Gerster, *The Art of the Maze*, Weidenfeld and Nicolson, 1990; Seven Dials, 2000.
Fisher, Adrian, and Howard Loxton, *Secrets of the Maze*, Thames and Hudson, 1997.
Kern, Hermann, *Through the Labyrinth* (translation), Prestel, 2000.
Kraft, John, *The Goddess in the Labyrinth*, Abo Akademi (Abo, Finland), 1985.
Matthews, W. H. *Mazes and Labyrinths*, Longmans, Green, 1922; re-issue Dover (New York), 1970.
Saward, Jeff, *Magical Paths*, Mitchell Beazley, 2003.
See also the periodical *Caerdroia*, ed. Jeff Saward, 53 Thundersley Grove, Thundersley, Benfleet, Essex, SS7 3EB, UK.

The Jubilee Maze or 'Hedge Puzzle' at Symonds Yat (West), in the Wye Valley, has a museum attached to it with much historical and visual material.

ACKNOWLEDGEMENTS

The publishers gratefully acknowledge the hel given by Adrian Fisher and Jeff Saward in th preparation of this guide.

All photographs kindly supplied by Adrian Fishe Maze Design except for
Jeff Saward pp. 4, 9 top, 11 top, 12 left, 14 lef 17 right, 22 left, 27, 37,
Skyscan p. 46.

Cover illustration by Andrew Jamieson.

Published by Wessex Books 2003
Reprinted 2010

Text © Geoffrey Ashe

Designed by Jane Drake

Design © Wessex Books 2003

ISBN 1-903035-14-7

Printed in India by Imprint Digital